Moving from Broken to Beautiful® through Forgiveness

Book 3
MOVING FROM BROKEN TO BEAUTIFUL® SERIES

YVONNE ORTEGA

Evelyn,
May God richly bless
you and your husband.

Yvonne
6/2/2016

Endorsements

"I love this book. It is thoughtful, inspiring, and a true gift to those who are experiencing feelings of persistent unforgiveness in their own lives. I love Yvonne's examples, the fact that it is Bible-based and that she offers affirmations, a summary of the main points for each chapter, and a space for keeping notes while reading."

Rev. Dr. Kitty Boitnott, NBCT
Boitnott Coaching, LLC

"The injured woman who thinks she's been irreparably damaged will be inspired to follow Yvonne Ortega's lead to submit to God and to 'plan a new and better life' in this box-seat version of Yvonne's journey through forgiveness. I found myself wondering if she had read my mind or eavesdropped on my personal conversations each time she described her own struggles with pardoning what would be punishable in a court of law. An honest, compelling, and challenging read!"

Sherry Boykin
Author, But-Kickers: *Growing Your Faith Bigger Than Your "But!"*

"After reading this work of art, I am convinced that this truly is a letter from God, written through Yvonne. The words felt as if they were written specifically for me, and I found myself sitting in shock at how her thoughts resonated with my own. The pages brought me to laughter and tears, through self-conviction and self-compassion. All I can say is, 'THANK YOU, YVONNE,' for persevering through such a journey and allowing God to use you and your testimony to inspire the rest of us. This book is nothing short of life changing. If you're ready to let go of the anger and grief and to build the life you have been missing out on, this is a must read."

Courtney Buzzell
Owner, Proximo Marketing Strategies LLC
President, Peninsula Women's Network

"*Moving from Broken to Beautiful® through Forgiveness* not only provides powerful messaging for your personal journey of forgiveness, it also opens a pathway of learning for all organizations that are in the process of rebuilding a broken culture. Yvonne's insight on the importance of repairing trust, ensuring well-being, building respect in relationships are the stepping stones of driving engagement and shaping a positive organizational culture. The one area that is not addressed during culture change that is so desperately needed and Yvonne brought to the forefront is forgiveness. Thank you, Yvonne, for giving me a WOW moment."

Dawn M. Cacciotti, SPHR HCS SHRM-SCP
Owner, HR Consultant
EngageHRnow – 'Get them to Great'

"The journey from forgiveness to freedom is one that Yvonne Ortega knows well. She shares practical ways to walk through the dark while showing you the light at the end of the tunnel. Yvonne doesn't pretend it is easy because she has been there. As you release the hold of those who have hurt you, what better person to lead you to what God promises?"

Jeanne Doyon
Pausing to See God Clearly
Writer, Speaker & Teacher

"*In Moving from Broken to Beautiful® through Forgiveness*, Yvonne Ortega gives you a blueprint to develop your personalized plan to work toward forgiveness. Yvonne serves as your guide and partner in the journey by sharing her stories, affirmations, and scriptural references. This book empowers you to move forward toward a new, successful life."

Angela L. Edwards, PMP, PCC, PMI-ACP
Castle Thunder Consulting, LLC

"Yvonne Ortega has written a beautiful and touching book on one of life's most difficult challenges: forgiveness. In *Moving from Broken to Beautiful® through Forgiveness*, Yvonne shares her own story and demonstrates her understanding and compassion. For everyone who needs to forgive someone in their life, this book is a God send."

Cathy Fyock, CSP
The Book Business Strategist

"This book will make a difference in the lives of the readers. It will be a healing balm for hurting people. The stories, questions, Scriptures, quotes, and prayers are salves for both open wounds and the hurts that have become scars."

Carolyn Knefely
Co-Director of Christian Communicators

"In *Moving from Broken to Beautiful® through Forgiveness*, author Yvonne Ortega has compiled one of the most complete and easily understood manuals on forgiveness that I've ever come across. This is a much-needed book for so many these days, and it certainly ministered to me as I read it. The clear and precise organization of the book lends itself to both individual or group reads. I can't recommend it enough to anyone who struggles with forgiveness issues."

Kathi Macias
Award-winning author of more than 50 books

"*Moving from Broken to Beautiful® through Forgiveness*, like its author, packs lots of power in a small package. Those who have suffered abuse in any form will love this book, filled with practical steps and encouragement to help readers move from pain, brokenness, and defeat to health, hope, and victory."

Marti Pieper
Author, Collaborative Writer, Editor

"Incredibly relatable! Yvonne's loving guidance through the process of forgiveness is one of great compassion and genuine support. Reading the pages, her tone is conversational, speaking directly into your heart, encouraging your healing. We have each been through at least one experience or relationship that requires healing. This book lovingly supports that innermost healing. This is a must-read, and a must-share book."

Sheryl Roush
Speaker, Speaking Coach, 17-time author, including *Heart of a Woman*

"With *Moving from Broken to Beautiful®️ through Forgiveness*, you will have Yvonne Ortega as your own personal companion through the process of forgiveness. Yvonne's stories will give you the confidence that you, too, can forgive others and enjoy the peace and freedom that follow! You will understand more fully what forgiveness is not and what it really is. The interactive exercises, affirmations, Scripture readings and prayers will help you more effectively come to grips with forgiveness in your own heart and life."

Glenna Salsbury, CSP, CPAE
Author of *The Art of the Fresh Start*
Professional Speaker
Past President of the National Speakers Association

"Reading Yvonne's book, *Moving from Broken to Beautiful®️ through Forgiveness* was like walking on 'the yellow brick road' to joy and peace. Needing to forgive or be forgiven is a universal life reality for everyone born into the earth. Yvonne masterfully takes a reader by the hand in friendship and sincerity, and with Godly wisdom shows you that a 'happily ever after' is not a fairytale."

Laura Seibert
Toastmasters International District 66 Division D
Director 2015-2016
Speaker, Author of *God Is*

"With first-hand knowledge of one who has experienced the pain, horror, and undeserved shame of abuse, gossip, or divorce, Yvonne Ortega understands the destructive power of unforgiveness. It's a cancer that eats at the heart and crushes the soul of believers and unbelievers alike.

But her advice is more than empty promises offering counterfeit peace by the simple recitation of written words. Instead, the reader is led to a place of transparency before the Father, accepting the double-edged truth that life isn't fair and revenge never heals. Ortega's step-by-step process can truly take you from broken to beautiful through the power of forgiveness."

Vonda Skelton
Speaker and author
Founder and Co-Director of Christian
Communicators

"I've learned that if you're holding a grudge, that grudge is also holding you. It's holding you back from everything you could have been and done. Yet Yvonne Ortega's book, *Moving from Broken to Beautiful*® *through Forgiveness*, provides the solution. Through her heartfelt stories and her amazing journey, Yvonne shows how forgiveness leads to true freedom. This is more than a book. It's a movement."

Craig Valentine
1999 Toastmasters World Champion of Public Speaking

"Forgiveness is one of the most powerful acts toward personal wholeness that we can experience in our life. It helps heal sickness and disease, heartache and trouble and other burdens and maladies of the spirit. This book is one of the easiest to understand, and most progressive and comprehensive books on forgiveness that you can read and tell others about. Digesting this book can dispel the ravages of anger, rage and defeat in your personal and business life and the life of your family as you share these truths with those you love."

Dr. Thelma Wells (Mama T)
CEO, That A Girl Enrichment Tours and A Woman of God Ministries
Author of 40 books including *Don't Give In, God Wants You To Win!*

"No one shares her heart and life's testimonies in the same open, funny, yet frank way that Sis Yvonne shares her pathway to forgiveness. *Moving from Broken to Beautiful® through Forgiveness* gives every reader the insight--if they are ready for it—to really be free of their 'broken pieces.' God's grace shines through in Sis Yvonne's writings and you know she wants to lead others through this journey and move them from broken to beautiful. Let her take your hand, Dear Reader, I did! Sit back, with a nice cup of herbal tea and just enjoy her words of wisdom."

Renee West
Executive Director, Legal Shield
Founder, Connecting the Dots Power Group, (Faith-based Marketplace Ministry)

Unless otherwise indicated, Scripture quotations are
taken from the *Holy Bible, New International Version®*.
NIV®. Copyright © 1973, 1978, 1984, 2011 by
Biblica, Inc.™ Used by permission of Zondervan. All
rights reserved worldwide. www.zondervan.com

Scripture quotations labeled ESV are from *The Holy
Bible, English Standard Version®*, copyright © 2001 by

Disclaimer

In loving memory of my mother,
Carlotta Ortega, who forgave me for moving away.
Also in loving memory of my son,
Brian,
His journey ended at a tender age.

Contents

Part Five: Let the Journey Begin: The Steps of Forgiveness

Acknowledgments

This book is not a one-woman product. You wouldn't be reading it if it were.

My international online writers' group—Geneva Iijima and Wendy Marshall—critiqued my manuscript from start to finish.

Sherry Boykin, Teri, Calhoun, Jeanne, Doyon, Angela Edwards, Carolyn Knefely, Kathy Pope, Karen Schlender, Dr. Sandra Sessoms-Penny and Renee West read the rough draft of this book and gave me their valuable feedback.

Glenna Salsbury, CSP, CPAE, encouraged me to share my message of hope at her Authentic You Retreat, which I attended twice.

Sheryl Roush, an Accredited Speaker and my business speaking coach, continued to tell me not to take on more than I could handle. Each time I considered another project or position, she would say, "Do you know what's involved in that?" After I answered her, she would say, "And what else?" She would ask me, "And what else?" at least three or four times. By then, I knew I couldn't take on one more responsibility. I wouldn't have finished this book without Sheryl. I can still hear Sheryl saying, "And what else?"

Cathy Fyock, my writing coach, gave the writers' group writing prompts each session via webinar and told us to link the prompt to our writing topic. I did mine on forgiveness. She also had two writing contests over the Christmas season: one to see who wrote the most words and another to see who finished the rough draft of their manuscript by January 11, 2016. I entered both contests. Cathy dangled prizes over us and hooked me. I completed the most words and finished my rough draft by January 11.

Craig Valentine, my speaker coach and the one who co-facilitated the World Class Speaking Coach class, encouraged me to share my story and taught me how in his speaker boot camps and through his products.

Numerous Toastmasters clubs allowed me to present speeches from the book chapters at their meetings.

Dr. Thelma Wells (Mama T) challenged me to write my story.

My endorsers, Kitty Boitnott, Sherry Boykin, Courtney Buzzell, Dawn Cacciotti, Jeanne Doyon, Angela Edwards, Cathy Fyock, Carolyn Knefely, Kathi Macias, Marti Pieper, Sheryl Roush, Glenna Salsbury, Laura Seibert, Vonda Skelton, Craig Valentine, Dr. Thelma Wells (Mama T), and Renee West endorsed my book before publication.

Dr. Caroline Savage from Trinity Press International edited my book.

The staff at Trinity Press International guided me in the process from manuscript to published book and e-book.

My friends in the Advanced Writers and Speakers Association (AWSA), my AWSA mastermind group, the Christian Communicators (CC), my church and my Women's Ministry Bible Study prayed for me.

My friends in my aqua classes listened to my updates on my manuscript and encouraged me.

I don't like cold weather, snow and ice, but that weather kept me indoors and at work on the manuscript. What else could I do when all activities were cancelled and the gym was closed?

My late mother was my best friend, my cheerleader, and my encourager. When I wrote my first book, she took it everywhere she went to show it off. I miss her so much, but her words of encouragement still linger in my mind and rest in my heart.

My dad has supported all my endeavors in education, speaking, and writing. I told him I wanted him to be proud of me. He said, "I already am proud of you."

And finally, dear readers, thank you for reading this book.

Introduction

I congratulate you, dear reader, for picking up this book on forgiveness. You show courage and a positive attitude. It took a few years before I would pick up a book on forgiveness.

Perhaps you're sick of feeling angry or depressed. Maybe a family member, a dear friend, or a coworker told you a while back that you needed to forgive someone who hurt you.

On the other hand, maybe a well-meaning person bought this book for you in hopes that you would not only read it but also do the interactive activities. You might have wanted to toss the book in the trash, burn it in your fireplace, or take it to the next bonfire. I understand. I remember exchanging a book someone thought I needed for a CD of soothing instrumental music. I took satisfaction in "showing" that person who was in charge of my recovery.

You may be scared to read a book on forgiveness. I empathize with you. You may think I will push you into doing something you don't want to do. You may think I will make you feel guilt and shame for not forgiving. Perhaps you wonder if I understand your pain. I may not understand your specific pain, but I've been through enough of my own to realize the trauma of it. So please relax. I won't do any of those things to you.

Maybe you think I'm a legalist like the Pharisees and Sadducees and will put a burden on you I've never carried or will carry. I'm not a legalist, and I carried the burden of traveling through the desert of unforgiveness for many years. I should have made the Guinness World Records because of the time it took me to make my way through the desert of unforgiveness.

Perhaps you read the table of contents or leafed through the pages of this book. Then you wondered if you would have enough tissue for the tears that might come. When I started the process of forgiveness, I did it kicking, stomping, and crying. Later, I allowed myself to face the full force of the pain, and I shed enough tears to fill the Atlantic Ocean. I never ran out of tissue. If you do and can't afford more, a kind person will buy you some. You can always put it on your Christmas or birthday list.

Right now, you may wish the pain from the offense and the offender would go away. I remember the times I wished a magic potion or trick would take away the pain from an offense or erase it from my memory. I prayed that the offender would go away. I also prayed he would die. That didn't happen, but God had a better plan. I sensed his power and presence to help me. Other times I felt God's comfort and assurance that good would come from it. I never dreamed it would be a book or speaking engagements on forgiveness. I have no idea what God will do for you, but God is in the miracle business. His do-overs or makeovers exceed your wildest dreams. Hang on and look forward to the future.

I may not have covered all your thoughts and feelings about forgiveness but hopefully enough for you to read on.

I have used the masculine pronoun, "he," in reference to the offender or perpetrator. I understand that women also hurt other people. However, for the sake of simplicity or flow in reading, I avoided writing "he or she" and "his or her" over and over.

Rather than go through this book alone, you can invite a friend or a coworker to join you. You can support and encourage each other. If the person you would like to ask doesn't live in the same area you do, you can communicate via phone, FaceTime, or Skype. Technology makes so many methods possible.

This book lends itself to a weekly small discussion or support group.

Consider that as one of your options and invite more than one friend or coworker to join you. You may even set up a private page on Facebook for your group. If you do, let me know. Please invite me so that I can drop in and encourage you.

However you decide to embark on your forgiveness journey, I wish you God's richest blessings.

To help you get the most from this book, I offer the following suggestions:

1. Buy a notebook or a blank journal to do the interactive activities at the end of every chapter.
2. Each chapter contains an anecdote or two. As you read them, apply them to your life.
3. At the end of each chapter, you will find three activities. You can do them alone, with a friend, or with a child of a suitable age.
4. After the activities, you will see the affirmations. You can write the affirmations on

sticky notes to place on a kitchen cupboard, your desk, or the bathroom mirror. Repeat them every time you see those sticky notes.

5. Next come the reading and the prayer. You can highlight, underline, or draw a circle around the readings in your Bible. If you'd rather not mark your Bible, you can write them on 3 x 5 cards to carry in your pocket or purse. Memorize and meditate on the readings.

6. You can say the prayer that is there alone or with someone else. Perhaps you prefer to write your own. That's fine too.

7. The journal pages are for your own use. If you'd rather not write in your book, you can use the notebook or journal you buy per the first suggestion.

8. The additional affirmations and readings will further help you internalize the message of this book.

9. If you have a personal computer or one at work, you can use the affirmations or readings as a screen saver and change them each week.

10. Perhaps music helps you express your thoughts and feelings. Write a song or a TV commercial for your favorite affirmations or readings. Your children may help you write a rap for them.

11. If drama sparks your interest, you can write a skit to go with any chapter you choose.

12. Finally, remember you are doing this for yourself, your health, your peace, and your freedom.

Part One

The Good News: What Forgiveness Is Not

Chapter 1

Forgiveness Doesn't Mean the Person Gets away with Wrongdoing

"Before you embark on a journey of revenge, dig two graves."[1]

Confucius

When you hear the word, forgiveness, what do you think of? Do you think of family members who hurt you, a boss who treated you unfairly, or a neighbor who mistreated your children? Do you consider forgiveness impossible? In the first section of this book, you will learn what forgiveness doesn't mean.

First, forgiveness doesn't mean the person gets away with wrongdoing. I didn't want to forgive my ex-husband. I thought if I did, he would get away with his abuse of our son and me. However, God says in Deuteronomy 32:35, "It is mine to avenge; I will repay." I wanted to help God do his job, but the Bible says God takes charge of those consequences. Only one God exists, and I'm not the one.

When I didn't see any consequences in my ex-husband's life right away, I reminded God to avenge our son and me by repaying my ex-husband. God didn't need my reminders. He knew what he promised.

I also wanted God to hurry and avenge us. I feared I would die and miss out on the satisfaction of witnessing that payback. My pastor said, "Yvonne, God will repay in his time, not yours."

My prayer for vengeance was for God to let my ex-husband die and burn in hell. Was that too much to ask? Funny thing, God never asked for my input, and he didn't answer that prayer to let my ex-husband die.

A few years later, God did repay my ex-husband. I won't give you the details of my ex-husband's consequences. Suffice it to say that consequences followed in every area of his life. God did keep his word.

God did far more than I could have ever imagined. My ex-husband's consequences reached such a point that death would have been easier. I felt sorry for him—just a little. Years later, I looked back and did feel sorry for him.

In the online September 15, 2013 issue of *Psychology Today²*, Karyn Hall, Ph.D. in her article, "Revenge: Will You Feel Better?" said, "Remember, while the anticipation of revenge may feel pleasurable, the actual carrying out of revenge brings little satisfaction and may create more problems and suffering. Acts of revenge do not repair trust or reestablish a sense of justice for both parties."

About ten years ago, a middle-aged man told me his wife had hurt him. He wouldn't say how, but he assured me she was not unfaithful to him. However, he felt justified in seeking revenge because she hurt him. He attempted to kill her, but his gun didn't go off. In terror, she left him and filed for divorce.

"Remember, while the anticipation of revenge may feel pleasurable, the actual carrying out of revenge brings little satisfaction and may create more problems and suffering."

As he and I talked over the months, he told me about the times he had been unfaithful and abusive to his wife. I pointed out that he hurt her, but she never tried to kill him. Instead she trusted God to keep his word and to repay her husband.

Years ago, my neighbor's husband committed adultery. His wife felt devastated. In retaliation, she also committed adultery. In her mind, they were even, and she felt justified. She later admitted to a close friend that revenge didn't make her feel better. She and her husband never rebuilt the trust in their marriage. They missed out on the happiness that might have been theirs if she hadn't sought revenge but had allowed God to repay her husband.

I talked at least a dozen times with a woman who refused to forgive a family member for sexually abusing her. She insisted that if she forgave him, he would get away with his criminal behavior. Her heart hardened with bitterness and resentment. She saw every man as an evil person, who lived to exploit women.

She was so full of anger that she decided no man would ever hurt her again. However, she shot an innocent man because he broke up with her. Vengeance didn't make her feel better. She regretted her desire to get even, but it was too late. The man died from the gunshot wound, and she received a long prison sentence.

Maybe you feel afraid to forgive an offender because you think that person will get away with wrongdoing. Maybe you struggle with a desire for revenge or wish God would hurry and repay the wrong. I encourage you to forgive. The offender will not get away with wrongdoing. God will repay in his time, not yours.

Chapter 1 Activities

- Journal about your thoughts and emotions in regard to the person who offended you.
- Spend your time and energy on daily exercise, hobbies, family, and friends.
- Make a list of the pros and cons of not seeking revenge.

Chapter 1 Affirmations

- I trust God to keep his word that vengeance is his.
- I don't waste my time and energy thinking of ways to repay an offender.
- I feel better if I avoid vengeance.

Chapter 1 Reading and Prayer

- "Do not take revenge, my dear friends, but leave room for God's wrath, for it is written: 'It is mine to avenge; I will repay,' says the Lord" (Romans 12:19).
- "Do not repay anyone evil for evil. Do not be overcome by evil, but overcome evil with good" (Romans 12:17, 21).
- "Vindicate me in your righteousness, LORD my God; do not let them gloat over me" (Psalm 35:24).

*Dear God, I'm so angry
I want to hurt that person the way he hurt me.
Help me to trust you and wait
for you to repay the evil done to me.*

Amen.

Chapter 1 Journal   **Date:** _____

Example: I don't want to forgive _____ because I fear he'll get away with what he did.

_____

_____

_____

_____

_____

_____

_____

_____

_____

_____

_____

_____

_____

_____

_____

_____

_____

_____

_____

_____

_____

_____

_____

_____

_____

_____

_____

_____

_____

Chapter 2
Forgiveness Doesn't Mean You Minimize, Deny, or Rationalize What Happened

"When you forgive, you in no way change the past - but you sure do change the future."[1]

Bernard Meltzer

Secondly, I learned forgiveness doesn't mean you minimize, deny, or rationalize what happened. Before the divorce, I never knew what my husband would do next. We had been married less than 24 hours when we left Myrtle Beach. He knew how much I loved that city, my friends, and my apartment by the beach. He knew how hard it was for me to leave and move with him to Boston. As we left Myrtle Beach, he said, "Look back, Yvonne. You'll never see Myrtle Beach again."

The smirk on his face and the mocking tone of his voice made me feel disrespected. I cried and couldn't understand why he would say something so insensitive to his new bride. He didn't try to console me or apologize for what he said. What happened to the nice man I married? I felt as if I were no longer a person but property he didn't need to respect. Although I should have confronted him, I said nothing and held in the shock and pain. That incident was a warning sign, but I denied it. I was in love and couldn't bear to face it. Unfortunately, the message he received was that I would tolerate his mean behavior.

I wish you could have been with me that same day when we stopped at a restaurant for dinner and ordered steak fondue. You would have smelled the sizzling pieces of steak in the fondue pot. You would have seen me gaze with love into my husband's eyes. You would have noticed he kept eating one piece of steak after another. But every time I looked into the fondue pot, the piece of steak on my fork was raw. Eventually you would have caught him as he placed my cooked piece of meat on his fork and put a raw one on mine. You would have heard me say, "Hey, what are you doing?"

Sadly, you would have heard him laugh. You would have noticed he never apologized for that incident either. Unfortunately, I still said nothing and held in more shock and pain. Once again, he received the message that I would tolerate his abuse. What kind of a person would do that? How could he be so selfish? Didn't he have a conscience? Once again, I felt as if I were property he didn't need to respect. Looking back, I see the warning signs I ignored.

After the honeymoon, we moved into our apartment. I asked him to take out the trash. He screamed, "My father never took out the trash. My mother always did it."

A little spunk in me surfaced, and I said, "I'm not your mother. You should have married her."

Over the years, his abuse became worse. On another occasion I was in the shower. My husband pulled the shower curtain back and asked, "What are you doing?"

"I'm taking a shower." I closed the shower curtain. Surely he could figure that out.

He pulled the shower curtain back a second time, and I closed it again. I didn't want water all over the floor. I would end up mopping it.

When I got out of the shower, he said, "There are other things besides karate."

He mentioned karate because I participated in a karate class.

He pointed to my eyes and my jugular vein and said, "You're powerless against a mad dog like me."

My husband's behavior was abusive and inexcusable. Because of his escalating abuse over the years, I ended up with a diagnosis of posttraumatic stress disorder.

Forgiveness will not change the reality of your offender's sinful behavior or his crimes.

If you've suffered from domestic violence, your husband's infidelity, or his pornography, it is bad. Perhaps you've endured his gambling, his substance abuse, or his financial chaos, it is bad. You don't have to pretend it isn't terrible or rationalize it in order to forgive him.

Perhaps you've suffered from sexual abuse, harassment on the job, or some other trauma. You don't have to deny, minimize, or rationalize it. Forgiveness will not change the reality of your offender's sinful behavior or his crimes.

In his book, *Total Forgiveness Revised and Updated*, R. T. Kendall says, "In the New Testament, Jesus forgave the woman found in adultery, but he did not approve of what she did. He told her, 'Leave your life of sin' (John 8:11)."[2]

Beth Moore in her Bible study, *Children of the Day*, says,

"Please note that enduring boldly for Christ does not mean allowing someone to abuse you. If you are being beaten, I implore you to get help immediately and refuse to rationalize an abuser's actions. Paul and Silas didn't sit quietly after their beating even though they'd been persecuted for the cause of Christ. They called out the wrongdoing and voiced the violation of their rights. Look for yourself in Acts 16:37. The Bible's idea of submission is for the sake of order, and those in positions of authority are charged by God to protect the people entrusted to them. An abusive authority figure is flagrantly outside the will of God and should and must be courageously reported. Otherwise, it is highly unlikely that you will be the last victim. Call the National Domestic Violence hotline at 1-800-799-7233."[3]

I encourage you to avoid minimization, denial, or rationalization. As a human being with dignity, you have the freedom and the right to call the behavior what it is and nothing less. If you need to call the National Domestic Violence hotline, for your own safety do so on someone else's phone but not on your own. That way your abuser won't find the hotline number on your phone log.

Chapter 2 Activities

- Journal your thoughts and emotions about minimization or denial of another person's inappropriate language or misbehavior.
- Draw a picture or cut out pictures from a magazine that demonstrate your strength and courage to stand up for the truth.
- Practice by yourself in front of a mirror as you talk out loud about the reality of an offender's sinful behavior or his crimes.

Chapter 2 Affirmations

- I won't minimize, deny, or rationalize a person's behavior.
- I face the truth of an offender's behavior.
- I can face reality and still forgive.

Chapter 2 Reading and Prayer

- "And you will know the truth, and the truth will set you free" (John 8:32 ESV).
- "Do not lie to each other, since you have taken off your old self with its practices and have put on the new self, which is being renewed in knowledge in the image of its Creator" (Colossians 3:9-10).
- "But speaking the truth in love, let us grow in every way into Him who is the head—Christ" (Ephesians 4:15 HCSB).

Dear God, you know fear has kept me
from facing the truth.
For years, I believed the lie
that if I expose the truth
I haven't forgiven _____.
Please help me avoid denial, minimization, or rationalization.

Amen.

Chapter 2 Journal   **Date:** _____

_____

_____

_____

_____

_____

_____

_____

_____

_____

_____

_____

_____

_____

_____

_____

_____

_____

Yvonne Ortega

_____

_____

_____

_____

_____

_____

_____

_____

_____

_____

_____

_____

_____

_____

_____

Chapter 3
Forgiveness Doesn't Mean You Forget What Happened

"Forgiving does not erase the bitter past.
A healed memory is not a deleted memory.
Instead, forgiving what we cannot forget creates a new way to
remember. We change the memory of our past into a hope for
our future."[1]

Lewis B. Smedes

If you want to start a heated argument among
Christians, ask them, "Does forgiveness mean you
forget what happened?" Some Christians believe you
have to forget in order to forgive. Do you believe
that? Others believe you can forgive, but you won't
forget. Perhaps you hold that opinion.

The Bible tells us to forgive in several Scriptures.
For example, Matthew 6:14 says, "For if you forgive
other people when they sin against you, your heavenly
Father will also forgive you."

Luke 6:37 says, "Do not judge, and you will not be judged. Do not condemn, and you will not be condemned. Forgive, and you will be forgiven."

Ephesians 4:32 says, "Be kind and compassionate to one another, forgiving each other, just as in Christ God forgave you." We are to forgive. However, the Bible never tells us to forgive and forget. Forgiveness doesn't mean we forget what happened.

If I had forgotten the incidents of escalating abuse in my marriage and stayed for more, I'm convinced my husband would have killed both me and our son, or we would have killed him in self-defense.

Years ago, a woman went to her pastor to tell him about her husband's physical abuse and threats to kill her. The pastor counseled her to stay and win her husband by her submission. She returned to the home as if it were a safe place. She ignored her husband's previous history of abuse and threats to kill her. Her husband shot her as he said he would, and she ended up a quadriplegic.

A young woman once told me, "I forgave the neighbor who sexually abused me as a child, but I didn't forget. If I had forgotten and played in his yard or gone back into his home, he would have sexually abused me again."

After years of enduring her husband's countless affairs, "Kristina" divorced her husband. She said, "Every time I caught Pete in an affair, he would tell me how much he loved me. He would cry and promise never to get involved with another woman again."

"Forgiving my perpetrator didn't mean suddenly shrugging my shoulders, muttering 'OK, I forgive,' and going on as if those things didn't happen. They did happen. And they took a terrible toll on my life."

Kristina bought a small home, worked full-time, pursued her hobbies, and became involved in church activities. One year later, Pete begged her to remarry him. He said, "I've changed, Kristina. I love you, and I'll never be unfaithful to you again." With tears running down his cheeks and flowers for her in his hands, he continued, "I've learned my lesson. You'll see. Just give me another chance."

He admitted to a mutual friend that he had not gone through counseling during the year they were divorced. He hadn't joined a recovery group, hadn't journaled, and didn't have a mentor or an accountability partner. He simply insisted he had changed. She had no proof that he had. However, she chose to forget about his countless affairs and the empty promises he'd made to her in the past.

She hung on to a false hope and remarried her former husband. Six months later, she discovered he was having an affair with another woman. Kristina suddenly remembered the years of putting up with Pete's numerous affairs and his empty promises. She divorced him again. Months later, she said, "I forgave him, Yvonne, but I won't forget this time. I don't ever want to go through the devastation of his infidelity again."

In her Bible study, *Breaking Free: Making Liberty in Christ a Reality in Life*, Beth Moore says, "Forgiving my perpetrator didn't mean suddenly shrugging my shoulders, muttering 'OK, I forgive,' and going on as if those things didn't happen. They did happen. And they took a terrible toll on my life."[2]

If you forget what happened, you may place yourself in a dangerous situation and experience further harm such as more financial exploitation, domestic violence, or sexual assault.

Forgiveness doesn't mean you forget what happened. It does mean you don't dwell on the offense day and night and allow it to take over your life.

R. T. Kendall, the pastor of Westminster Chapel in London, England for twenty-five years, wrote forty books. He is well known internationally as a speaker and teacher. In his book, *Total Forgiveness Revised and Updated*, R.T. Kendall says, "Literally to forget may not be realistic. It is usually impossible to forget meaningful events in our lives, whether positive or negative . . . It is actually a demonstration of greater grace when we are fully aware of what occurred—and we still choose to forgive."[3]

Chapter 3 Activities

- Journal about an offense that broke your heart.
- Make a list of the benefits of forgiveness but not forgetting.
- Role-play with a trusted friend, mentor, or counselor in which you describe the effects an offense had on you.

Chapter 3 Affirmations

- I can forgive.
- I don't need to forget the offense to forgive.
- I set a boundary to avoid further danger.

Chapter 3 Reading and Prayer

- "The prudent see danger and take refuge, but the simple keep going and pay the penalty" (Proverbs 22:3).
- "The gullible believe anything they're told; the prudent sift and weigh every word" (Proverb 14:15 Message).
- "Foolish dreamers live in a world of illusion; wise realists plant their feet on the ground" (Proverbs 14:18 Message).

Dear God, help me not to be consumed by past hurts.
Give me the strength to forgive.
But I want to be prudent,
not gullible or a foolish dreamer.

Amen.

Chapter 3 Journal   **Date:** _____

_____

_____

_____

_____

_____

_____

_____

_____

_____

_____

_____

_____

_____

_____

_____

_____

_____

Yvonne Ortega

_____

_____

_____

_____

_____

_____

_____

_____

_____

_____

_____

_____

_____

_____

_____

Chapter 4
Forgiveness Doesn't Mean You Forgive the Person Right away

"Forgiveness is a process, not an event."[1]

Dr. Tian Dayton

Forgiveness is not like instant oatmeal, instant coffee, or instant tea. Dr. Charles Stanley is a pastor in Atlanta, GA and the New York Times best-selling author of more than sixty books. In his sermon series on *Anger and Forgiveness*, *Letting Go of Anger: Part 4*, Dr. Charles Stanley said, "Forgiveness will not always be easy or quick."[2]

Dr. Tian Dayton is a clinical psychologist and author. In *Huffpost Healthy Living* on May 25, 2015, Dr. Dayton said, "Forgiveness is a process, not an event. It takes work; it takes time. And it doesn't happen all at once nor does it happen completely, at least for a while. It has stages, and there can be many roadblocks along the way."[3]

I felt better after reading those two articles online. They confirmed my own struggle with forgiveness. At first, I didn't want to forgive my ex-husband. Why should I? He hurt our son and me. I had a mental record of everything he said and did wrong. My written list covered several pages in my journal. I considered forgiveness impossible.

Once I decided to forgive my ex-husband, it took me years of work. Talk about obstacles! I would go along for a while and beam with a sense of progress. Then either he would be abusive, or something would trigger the memory of an incident from the past. My hurt would rise again, and I would feel like I was starting over.

For example, my ex-husband dragged out the divorce for four years. A year after it was final, he filed a state appeal apparently because he didn't agree with the judge's decision. That case would be heard in federal court, and I would have to hire a different lawyer, one who handled state appeals. When I received notice of his state appeal, I cried and said, "God, will that man never leave me alone? All I want is peace and quiet." I wished he were sick and dying or dead and buried. Then I could leave dandelions at his gravesite.

A coworker told me after her divorce she went through a long process to forgive her ex-husband. She said she used to wish he were dead, so she could dance on his grave. I laughed. I thought that was a fabulous idea and could picture myself dancing on my ex-husband's grave. I said, "Hey if your ex-husband and mine die at the same time, we can go together to the cemetery and dance on their graves."

As I worked on forgiveness, I reminded myself that I was doing the best I could and that forgiveness was a process.

I encourage you to take the time and effort you need to forgive an offender. Don't feel obligated to follow someone else's timetable. You don't need to feel guilty if you don't forgive a person as quickly as you heat instant oatmeal.

However, the next day, the next week, or the next month, the person can say or do something else offensive or a memory can surface that puts you right back in that same emotional turmoil. That's what I mean about the process of forgiveness.

Perhaps right now, you're wondering how that process fits in with Ephesians 4:26 that says, "'In your anger do not sin.' Do not let the sun go down while you are still angry."

As I struggled to forgive my ex-husband, I looked at that verse and said, "God, somewhere in the world the sun hasn't gone down yet."

An incident or an accumulation of them can trigger your anger and unforgiveness. You can talk and pray with a mentor, a friend, or a counselor about that trigger. You can ask God to help you through it and choose to let it go. In that moment, you know you have forgiven the person for everything that has happened up to that point. However, the next day, the next week, or the next month, the person can say or do something else offensive or a memory can surface that puts you right back in that same emotional turmoil. That's what I mean about the process of forgiveness.

Chapter 4 Activities
- Journal about your battle with forgiveness.
- Draw or cut pictures out of a magazine that depict your pain from the offender's words or actions. Talk about that pain with a trusted friend, mentor, or counselor.
- Find a song on YouTube that expresses your feelings about the amount of time it takes to forgive.

Chapter 4 Affirmations
- I forgive as I can.
- I don't push myself to completely forgive by a certain date.
- Another person's progress doesn't dictate mine.

Chapter 4 Reading and Prayer

- "And whenever you stand praying, if you have anything against anyone, forgive him, so that your heavenly Father will also forgive you your wrongdoing" (Mark 11:25 HCSB).
- "Have patience with all things, but chiefly have patience with yourself. Do not lose courage in considering your own imperfections but instantly set about remedying them– every day begin the task anew." ~ Francis de Sales[4]
- "Then Peter came to Jesus and asked, 'Lord, how many times shall I forgive my brother or sister who sins against me? Up to seven times?' Jesus answered, 'I tell you, not seven times, but seventy-seven times'" (Matthew 18:21-22). Note that the KJV says, "Seventy times seven."

Dear God, some days I feel like
I've completely forgiven the one who hurt me.
The next day something happens,
and I feel like
I'm on the emotional roller coaster again.
Help me not to give up on the process of forgiveness.

Amen.

Chapter 4 Journal   **Date:** _____

_____

_____

_____

_____

_____

_____

_____

_____

_____

_____

_____

_____

_____

_____

_____

_____

_____

_____

Chapter 5
Forgiveness Doesn't Mean You Immediately Trust the Offender

"Forgiveness does not create a relationship.
Unless people speak the truth about what they have done and
change their mind and behavior,
a relationship of trust is not possible."[1]

Wm. Paul Young, *The Shack*

Forgiveness doesn't mean you immediately trust the offending person. Trust is earned over time, not freely given. Second Corinthians 7:10 says, "Godly sorrow brings repentance." In *Vine's Complete Expository Dictionary of Old and New Testament Words*, to repent means "to change one's mind or purpose always . . . for the better." *Vine's Dictionary* also says that in the New Testament, repentance refers to sin, and "this change of mind involves both a turning from sin and a turning to God."

My husband would make promises to change, but

he wouldn't keep them. He said what he thought I wanted to hear but never showed godly sorrow. He didn't repent or change for the better. Instead he became worse. After he severely beat our son and pulled out a gun on me, I couldn't trust him. My husband told me he loved me, but I had heard that too many times. I was no longer naive.

After I filed for divorce, my husband told our son, "An alcoholic gets more forgiveness than I do." Rather than repent, he tried to make a confidante out of our child. He also tried to turn our son against me and use him to shame me or pressure me into forgiving and trusting him again.

In contrast, a former batterer once told me through tears, "Yvonne, I realized how much I hurt my wife. I decided if I really loved her, I could never hurt her again."

"How long ago was that?"

"Thirteen years ago, and I love her more today than I ever have. I can't even think of hurting her."

That's repentance, and he has regained his wife's trust. He earned her trust by changing his behavior for the better. He consistently showed her week after week, month after month, and year after year that he had turned from his sin of abuse and turned to God. He was no longer the abusive husband he once was.

"Larry" served a jail sentence of three months for a second DUI, driving under the influence of alcohol. He also had to pay a $500 fine. Upon his release from jail, he expected his wife "Jenny" to trust him immediately. When she didn't, he complained. "I've been sober for three months. I learned my lesson, and I promised Jenny I won't drink again."

I reminded Larry that he had been sober for three months because of his incarceration. I also reminded him that after his first DUI he told Jenny he had learned his lesson and promised not to drink again. "So what's different this time, Larry?"

He tapped my desk with his fingers and said, "This time I've really learned my lesson. This time I mean it. I won't drink again."

I smiled and handed Larry a list of AA meetings in the area and information on Celebrate Recovery. I suggested he get a sponsor, attend at least one meeting weekly, and work the twelve-step program. "Show your wife by your actions that you have learned your lesson and don't plan to drink again."

"You make it sound as if I'm on trial."

Perhaps your offender wants to shame you or pressure you into an immediate return of trust in him. You can forgive him, but that doesn't mean you trust him. He must earn your trust.

"In a way, you are, Larry. If you go out with your drinking buddies, the message to your wife is that you'll soon drink again."

Larry protested. "I can't afford to drink again." He leaned forward in his chair and said, "If I get a third DUI, I'll go to jail for a minimum of six months, pay a minimum fine of $1,000, and lose my driver's license indefinitely."

"All the more reason to carry out my suggestions to stay sober, get a sponsor, attend weekly meetings, and regain your wife's trust."

As Larry headed for the door, I said, "Remember that your driver's license is suspended for three years. If you want to earn Jenny's trust again, show her by your actions that you don't drink anymore and won't drive with a suspended license."

Perhaps your offender wants to shame you or pressure you into an immediate return of trust in him. You can forgive him, but that doesn't mean you trust him. He must earn your trust. He needs to show you he has changed for the better. He needs to consistently demonstrate to you that he has repented, that he has turned from sin, and turned to God.

Chapter 5 Activities

- Journal about your reasons for not immediately trusting your offender.
- Make a list of behaviors that would indicate your offender's change of mind and heart for the better.
- Accept the fact that your offender may be upset about having to regain your trust.

Chapter 5 Affirmations

- I love and respect myself enough not to jump into an immediate trust of an offender.
- I take my time to look for signs of the offender's repentance.
- I won't let an offender try to hurry me into trusting him again.

Chapter 5 Reading and Prayer

- "Like a broken tooth or a lame foot is reliance on the unfaithful in time of trouble" (Proverbs 25:19).

- "Do not trust a neighbor; put no confidence in a friend. Even with the woman who lies in your embrace guard the words of your lips. For a son dishonors his father, a daughter rises up against her mother, a daughter-in-law against her mother-in-law—a man's enemies are the members of his own household" (Micah 7:5-6).

- "The Lord is with me; I will not be afraid. What can mere mortals do to me? It is better to take refuge in the LORD than to trust in humans. It is better to take refuge in the LORD than to trust in princes" (Psalm 118:6, 8-9).

Dear God, I don't like conflict.
I prefer to have peace.
Peace at any price is not peace.
Help me remember that
And not rush into trusting an offender.

Amen.

Chapter 5 Journal   **Date:** _____

_____

_____

_____

_____

_____

_____

_____

_____

_____

_____

_____

_____

_____

_____

_____

_____

_____

Yvonne Ortega

Part Two

**The Tough News:
What God Says about Forgiveness**

Chapter 6
God Talks about Grievances

The individual who cultivates grievances, and who is perpetually
exacting explanations of his assumed wrongs, can only be
ignored, and left to the education of time and of development....
One does not argue or contend with the foul miasma that settles
over stagnant water one leaves it and climbs to a higher region,
where the air is pure and the sunshine fair.[1]

Lilian Whiting

In the process of moving from broken to
beautiful through forgiveness, you've looked at the
many things that are not part of forgiveness. Now
you will look at what God says in the Bible about
forgiveness. In Colossians 3:13, God says, "Bear with
each other and forgive whatever grievances you may
have against one another. Forgive as the Lord forgave
you."

I liked the first part of Colossians 3:13, "Bear with
each other." I was home in Virginia and my ex-

husband was on the other side of the world in the war zone. I didn't have to worry about bearing with him.

Do you know what God told me? "Pray for him."

"Really, God? Are you serious?" I prayed all right, "God, please don't let him come back from the war zone. It would be easier for our son and me without him. Let my ex-husband die and burn in hell." Was that too much to ask for?

In the quiet of my home, I sensed God whisper, "Yvonne, that's not what I meant. Now you pray for him."

> "And forgive whatever grievances you may have against one another."

Through clenched teeth and an overflow of tears, I knelt and prayed God would bless him. My <u>head</u> took over. My heart was unwilling because of the years of financial, verbal, emotional, and physical abuse.

I didn't like the next part of Colossians 3:13. It says, "And forgive whatever grievances you may have against one another." I wanted to pretend that part of the Bible verse wasn't there or that I never saw it. That didn't work. I reminded God of the terrible things my ex-husband said and did to our son and me. Surely, under those circumstances, God would allow exceptions to the rule. Wouldn't he? I attempted to scrutinize that part of the verse, as a biologist would study a bug under a microscope. The word, "whatever," blocked me. I hated to admit it, but God didn't leave me any loopholes.

Maybe you don't like that part of Colossians 3:13 either. Your grievances may be legitimate, but God doesn't leave you any exceptions. God longs to see you moving from broken to beautiful through forgiveness.

Colossians 3:13 also says, "Forgive as the Lord forgave you." I wasn't perfect. At the time of the divorce I had been a non-Christian more years than I had been a Christian. God had totally forgiven me. He didn't remind me of my past. God forgave me at great cost to his one and only Son Jesus Christ, who died on the cross for my sins. The cost of forgiveness would be my pride and letting go of anger. That would be nothing in comparison to the price Jesus paid. I didn't deserve forgiveness, but God forgave me anyway. Now God wanted me to do the same for my ex-husband. I cried, stomped, and screamed, "That's unfair. It's too painful. I can't do it."

I sensed God say, "Do you think it was fair for my Son Jesus to die for your sins? Don't you think his death on the cross was painful?"

"Now that you put it that way, God. What's a poor woman to do?"

> "Forgive as the Lord forgave you."

Let's look at Colossians 3:13 again, "Bear with each other and forgive whatever grievances you may have against one another. Forgive as the Lord forgave you." This Bible verse is not an invitation. It's a command. The verse says, "Forgive as the Lord forgave you." God doesn't provide exceptions or loopholes. He sets a high standard.

Perhaps right now, you're struggling because of the way your parents abused you as a child. Perhaps the struggle comes from the way your husband or a boss mistreated you. Perhaps the struggle comes from the way a neighbor or a babysitter hurt your children. You think you shouldn't have to forgive the person. No matter what you're thinking, you might as well tell God. He already knows anyway. He has your greater good in mind. God wants you moving from broken to beautiful through forgiveness.

Chapter 6 Activities

- Journal about a grievance you've held onto.
- Make a list of the pros and cons of letting go of that grievance.
- Listen to a classic hymn about forgiveness, such as "Grace Greater Than Our Sin" or to a more contemporary song, such as "Forgiveness" by Matthew West.

Chapter 6 Affirmations

- I can forgive as the Lord forgave me.
- I can forgive whatever grievances I have against another.
- I can move from broken to beautiful through forgiveness.

Chapter 6 Reading and Prayer

- "For the Lord God is a sun and shield; the Lord bestows favor and honor; no good thing does he withhold from those whose walk is blameless" (Psalm 84:11).

- "He [Jesus] replied, 'Blessed rather are those who hear the word of God and obey it'" (Luke 11:28).

- "Jesus replied, 'Anyone who loves me will obey my teaching. My Father will love them, and we will come to them and make our home with them. Anyone who does not love me will not obey my teaching. These words you hear are not my own; they belong to the Father who sent me'" (John 14:23-24).

*Dear God, I don't want to forgive
those who hurt me.
I can name dozens of reasons
they don't deserve my forgiveness.
But you can name dozens of reasons
I don't deserve your forgiveness.
The Scriptures say if I love you, I will obey you.
I do love you. Please help me forgive.*

Amen.

Chapter 6 Journal

Date: _____

_____

_____

_____

_____

_____

_____

_____

_____

_____

_____

_____

_____

_____

_____

_____

_____

_____

_____

_____

_____

_____

_____

_____

_____

_____

_____

_____

_____

_____

_____

_____

_____

Chapter 7
God Talks about Bitterness

"Bitterness is cancer-it eats upon the host.
It doesn't do anything to the object of its displeasure."[1]

Maya Angelou

I knew better than to choose bitterness and anger. I was not only a Christian but also a Bible teacher. However, instead of facing the reality of my marriage, I had denied, minimized, or rationalized incident after incident. I had held in my anger and unforgiveness for years, until those feelings overwhelmed me and gushed out like water from a fire hydrant.

In the midst of those terrible emotions, God spoke to me through the Bible. It says, "Get rid of all bitterness, rage and anger, brawling and slander, along with every form of malice. Be kind and compassionate to one another, forgiving each other, just as in Christ God forgave you" (Ephesians 4:31-

32).

My pastor preached a series on that same Bible passage. God continued to work on me and bring me closer to being able to forgive.

Somehow I had to obey God and forgive that man. How could I do it? The Bible also says, "With God all things are possible." I didn't want to forgive my ex-husband, but God changed my desires into his desires. I sensed God leading me to forgive my ex-husband.

"Get rid of all bitterness, rage and anger, brawling and slander, along with every form of malice."

Day after day for months, I would go to the beach with my Bible and journal. One time before I went to the beach, I had attended a workshop on domestic violence. The speaker said that boys who grew up in homes where they witnessed domestic violence were seven times more likely to become batterers. She called it "learned behavior." They didn't like the abuse growing up, but they became batterers anyway. They learned that violence was the way to control their wives or partners.

I recalled a conversation my ex-husband and I had when we were dating. He said, "My dad hit my mother almost every day. Once when I was little, I pulled on my dad's pant leg and said, "Don't hit Mommy.""

That conversation was a warning sign. Because of my lack of information about domestic violence at that time, I didn't recognize it. I also didn't see how his parents interacted with each other until a few years after our marriage.

My ex-husband learned from his father that it's okay for men to verbally, emotionally, and physically abuse their wives. His father taught him by his actions that men can do whatever they want and don't have to account for their actions. The women are supposed to accept it, and they better not dare complain.

My ex-husband's upbringing didn't excuse his behavior. As the speaker said at the workshop, some boys who witness abuse choose not to become batterers. My ex-husband made the decision to behave in an abusive manner, and he knew what he was doing was wrong.

How can I say he knew it? After I filed for divorce, he asked, "Was it the way I was behaving?"

Regardless of his decision and his understanding of wrongdoing, I had to account for my behavior. I chose to forgive him out of obedience to God.

This Bible passage doesn't change no matter how much others have hurt or disappointed you. When God says, "Get rid of all bitterness, rage and anger, brawling and slander," he means <u>all</u>. When God says, "along with every form of malice," he means <u>every</u> form. You can't allow exceptions to the rule. They'll get you in trouble every time. Trust me. I know.

In the Bible, God says, "Be kind and compassionate to one another, forgiving each other, just as in Christ God forgave you."

When God forgives you of your sins, he doesn't remind you of them. Therefore, God doesn't want you to throw a person's past wrongs in his face every time you see that person. That would leave you in emotional turmoil shackled to the person you refuse to forgive.

Chapter 7 Activities

- Journal about the meaning of the words, *all* and *every* in the Ephesians passage above.
- Make a list of all the times God forgave you.
- Listen to a traditional hymn or a contemporary song on forgiveness, kindness, or compassion, such as *The Great Physician* or *Mighty to Save* by Hillsong.

Chapter 7 Affirmations

- I will obey God and forgive my offender.
- I accept God's help to forgive my offender.
- I avoid exceptions to God's rule to forgive.

Chapter 7 Reading and Prayer

- "For if you forgive other people when they sin against you, your heavenly Father will also forgive you. But if you do not forgive others their sins, your Father will not forgive your sins" (Matthew 6:14-15).

- "Do not judge, or you too will be judged. For in the same way you judge others, you will be judged, and with the measure you use, it will be measured to you" (Matthew 7:1-2).

- "So in everything, do to others what you would have them do to you, for this sums up the Law and the Prophets" (Matthew 7:12).

Dear God, I need your help.
On my own, I can't forgive my offender.
I come up with a thousand reasons why I shouldn't.
Thank you for listening to my cry for help.

Amen.

Chapter 7 Journal   **Date:** _____

_____

_____

_____

_____

_____

_____

_____

_____

_____

_____

_____

_____

_____

_____

_____

_____

_____

_____

_____

_____

_____

_____

_____

_____

_____

_____

_____

_____

_____

_____

_____

_____

Part Three

Look What You're in for with Unforgiveness

Chapter 8
The Self-defeating Sacrifice of Unforgiveness

"A mind that opens its door to fears, doubts, grudges, jealousy and anger, compromises its peace in return."[1]

Edmond Mbiaka

Have you ever worried about what you would lose if you forgave? I did. I constantly asked myself several questions: "What will happen to me if I forgive? Will I lose my power, my identity, or my personality? Will people walk all over me? Will I be considered a fool, a doormat, or something worse?"

Those questions were and still are important. However, the most important question to ask is "What will happen to me if I don't forgive?"

First, let's look at the physical effects of unforgiveness. Years ago, I struggled to forgive my ex-husband. At that same time, I suffered from chronic back pain. I couldn't sleep at night and felt exhausted most of the time. My food didn't digest well, and I lost twenty pounds. I looked like a bag of bones. One day I ran into a friend who hadn't seen me in a while. He gasped in horror and said, "Yvonne, what happened to you? We're losing you."

I told him how horrible my ex-husband was. As he listened, he said, "Honey, you've got to let it go. Forgive the guy for your own good and move on."

Now I know he was right.

However, the most important question to ask is "What will happen to me if I don't forgive?"

Do you suffer from migraine headaches, ulcers, or colitis? What about high blood pressure, a heart attack, or a stroke? Maybe an eating disorder or substance abuse has a grip on you. A lack of forgiveness can cause any of those physical problems. However, please don't ignore them. Go to your doctor for a physical checkup and take good care of yourself.

Second, let's look at the emotional effects of unforgiveness. I sacrificed my emotional well-being to hold onto a grudge. I felt anxious, stressed, and depressed. When my depression hit an all-time low, I would no longer drive to Virginia Beach or to Gloucester because I would have to cross the bridge. I feared I would drive right off the bridge and drown. Suicide seemed like the only way out of the anxiety, stress, and depression.

Have you paid an emotional price because of
unforgiveness?

I withdrew from my friends and social events. One Sunday, Kendra came over and rang the doorbell until I opened the door. She said, "I've had enough of your isolation. No more. Get dressed to go to the singles' picnic. I won't leave this house without you."

At her insistence, I went and had a good time. I laughed for the first time in weeks.

Do you feel anxious, stressed, or depressed? Have you paid an emotional price because of unforgiveness? If your emotional handcuffs of unforgiveness could speak, they would say, "Please take me off. You're restricting my movement. Don't you have other bracelets that fit better?"

The third self-defeating sacrifice of unforgiveness is the spiritual effects. In 2 Corinthians 2:10-11, Paul says, "Anyone you forgive, I also forgive. And what I have forgiven—if there was anything to forgive—I have forgiven in the sight of Christ for your sake, in order that Satan might not outwit us. For we are not unaware of his schemes."

Does unforgiveness stand between you and God?

I can look back now and see that the real battle wasn't against my ex-husband. It was against Satan himself. I have a spiritual enemy, the devil who hates me. Satan's scheme was to hold me in bondage through unforgiveness. He also attempted to destroy my relationship with my heavenly Father and with anyone connected to the church. He almost succeeded. I nearly gave up my prayer life, Bible study, and church attendance.

My friend Kathy intervened. She said, "Yvonne, you have a choice to make. Your first choice is to continue to ride the spiritual roller coaster of unforgiveness. That will make you a puppet of Satan as you continue to fall for his schemes. Your second choice is to obey God and forgive."

Sometime later, I selected the second choice and obeyed God.

Maybe your spiritual communion with God is not what it used to be. Perhaps you've lost your joy. Perhaps your prayer life and Bible study deteriorate by the week. Does unforgiveness stand between you and God?

At the beginning of this chapter, like me, you might have wanted to know if you would lose your power, your identity, and your personality if you forgave. Like me, you might now see how much you lose if you don't forgive. I decided the price was too big. What have you decided?

Chapter 8 Activities

- Journal about the cost of unforgiveness in your life.
- Make a list of the pros and cons of forgiveness.
- Imagine a perfect day of peace.

Chapter 8 Affirmations

- Each day I take care of my physical health.
- Every day I'm emotionally stronger.
- I value my spiritual communion with God.

Chapter 8 Reading and Prayer

- "My son, pay attention to what I say; turn your ear to my words. Do not let them out of your sight, keep them within your heart; for they are life to those who find them and health to one's whole body" (Proverbs 4:20-22).

- "Blessed is the one who does not walk in step with the wicked or stand in the way that sinners take or sit in the company of mockers, but whose delight is in the law of the Lord, and who meditates on his law day and night. That person is like a tree planted by streams of water, which yields its fruit in season and whose leaf does not wither—whatever they do prospers" (Psalm 1:1-3).

- "I will never forget your precepts, for by them you have preserved my life" (Psalm 119:93).

Dear God, anger and bitterness wear me out.
I don't want to feel depressed anymore.
Help me obey you and live.

Amen.

Chapter 8 Journal   Date: _____

_____

_____

_____

_____

_____

_____

_____

_____

_____

_____

_____

_____

_____

_____

_____

_____

_____

Part Four

The Tougher News: How God Wants You to Treat Your Enemies

Chapter 9

Where Are You on the Forgiveness Scale?

"Always forgive your enemies; nothing annoys them so much."[1]

Oscar Wilde

"Oh my goodness! I think I'm going to throw up. God can't possibly want me to follow the example of Moses, can he? During my angry unforgiving days, I was reading Numbers 12 in the Bible. Aaron and Miriam, the brother and sister of Moses, were jealous of him. Numbers 12:13 says, "Miriam and Aaron began to talk against Moses because of his Cushite wife, for he had married a Cushite. 'Has the LORD spoken only through Moses?' they asked. 'Hasn't he also spoken through us?' And the LORD heard this."

Numbers 12:9 says, "The anger of the LORD burned against them, and he left them." Afterward Miriam's skin became white as snow with leprosy. Aaron admitted their sin to Moses and pleaded for mercy.

Moses could have said, "That's what you get for talking against God's anointed leader." Instead he begged God to heal Miriam, and God did so after telling Moses to confine her outside their camp for seven days.

"What? Only seven days? Where's the justice in this world?" I cried and stomped again. You see, time after time my ex-husband talked to our son about me. My son would get upset and come to me afterward. After talking about his father to him once, I had vowed that no matter what my ex did, I wouldn't do that again. I tried to be nice and that's the thanks I got!

Now through the passage in Numbers 12, God showed me I needed to intercede for my ex-husband. I would have preferred he got leprosy and kept it. That's why Moses was anointed, and I wasn't.

Can you identify with me? Is God talking to you through that passage? On a scale of 1-10, where are you on the forgiveness scale?

One day a "friend" called me and said, "Yvonne, why don't you pray for your ex-husband according to the first part of Romans 1:24: "Wherefore God also gave them up to uncleanness through the lusts of their own hearts" (KJV).

I did pray that way one day only, but God convicted me to stop that kind of prayer. I called my friend and said, "I can't do it. That's my son's father."

Another person called me and said, "Yvonne, why don't you pray that your ex-husband dies?" At that point, I realized that person was tempting me to sin. I cried as I told her, "I can't pray that way. That's my son's father. My son needs his love as much as he needs mine."

God had convicted me that no matter what people told me, I had to bless my ex-husband and pray for him. He did that through Luke 6:27-28: "But to you who are listening I say: Love your enemies, do good to those who hate you, bless those who curse you, pray for those who mistreat you."

That passage can make you angrier when you're in the throes of rage and unforgiveness, but with time and God's overflowing grace and strength you will get there. I understand if you don't want to accept those verses right now. I remember crying when I first read them. I told God, "I'm not among those who are listening. I can't stand those verses."

Again, I ask, "Where are you on the forgiveness scale?"

God showed me yet another passage about how to treat the enemy. Romans 12:20-21 says, "To the contrary, 'if your enemy is hungry, feed him; if he is thirsty, give him something to drink; for by so doing you will heap burning coals on his head.' Do not be overcome by evil, but overcome evil with good" (ESV). I liked the part about "[heaping] burning coals on his head," but I had to work on the rest of that passage.

Once in Sunday school, a friend brought up an incident that caused me to think about that passage from God's point of view. My friend said that as she walked out of the grocery store, she saw a woman in the parking lot take one of her keys and scrape a new car on the driver's side from the headlight to the taillight. The woman got into her car and drove past my friend. She memorized the license plate number and called the police. She later learned that woman's boyfriend had broken up with her and had a new girlfriend. In retaliation, the "key-scraping artist" had damaged his new car.

Okay. I got it. I could not be overcome by evil. Somehow I had to overcome evil with good.

As the Christmas season approached, a divorced coworker mentioned she would be going to her ex-husband's home on Christmas Day with the children. Her ex-husband had been unfaithful, divorced her, and married the other woman. My coworker said that for the sake of the children, she would take them to her ex-husband's home to celebrate Christmas and open presents there. She glowed as she told me how much that meant to the children, how that eliminated conflict, and brought peace instead. She had something I didn't.

One year, my ex-husband planned to be with our son through Christmas Eve. I would be with him starting on Christmas Day. Our son lived out of state. I booked my flight and then checked into a car rental. Imagine my delight when I found a special on a car rental. I thought about my coworker and called my ex-husband to inform him about the special. He thanked me for telling him. I told myself that I did it for our son. Hopefully that would mean more money his father would spend on him.

On Christmas Eve, I arrived mid-afternoon where my son was. God with his sense of humor had his father and me stay at the same hotel. When my son saw me, he said, "Mom, please come to Dad's room. He has all kinds of appetizers and snacks for Christmas Eve. Please, please come."

I admit fear of my ex-husband lacing the food with poison went through my head, but I went for the sake of our child. I also watched to see if he would eat the food first. When my ex-husband and our son weren't looking, I also moved the food around. My son smiled and chattered that evening as the three of us celebrated Christmas Eve together.

Memories of the cruel things my ex-husband said and did to us flashed through my mind. God in his goodness reminded me of what Jesus said to Peter in Matthew 16:23: "But he turned and said to Peter, 'Get behind me, Satan! You are a hindrance to me. For you are not setting your mind on the things of God, but on the things of man'" (ESV).

Perhaps horrible memories flash through your head too. I understand. It's not easy to obey God. The devil will do all he can to keep you stuck in the past.

Chapter 9 Activities

- Draw a scale from 1-10 and mark where you are on the forgiveness scale.
- Journal about where you would like to be on the forgiveness scale and why.
- Meditate on either Romans 12:20-21 or Matthew 16:23 in your favorite version of the Bible.

Chapter 9 Affirmations

- I will not be overcome with evil.
- I will overcome evil with good.
- I can move up on the forgiveness scale.

Chapter 9 Reading and Prayer

- "While they were stoning him, Stephen prayed, 'Lord Jesus, receive my spirit.' Then he fell on his knees and cried out, 'Lord, do not hold this sin against them.' When he had said this, he fell asleep [died]" (Acts 7:59-60).

- "But Moses sought the favor of the Lord his God. 'Lord,' he said, 'why should your anger burn against your people, whom you brought out of Egypt with great power and a mighty hand? Why should the Egyptians say, 'It was with evil intent that he brought them out, to kill them in the mountains and to wipe them off the face of the earth'? Turn from your fierce anger; relent and do not bring disaster on your people. Remember your servants Abraham, Isaac and Israel, to whom you swore by your own self: 'I will make your descendants as numerous as the stars in the sky and I will give your descendants all this land I promised them, and it will be their inheritance forever.' Then the Lord relented and did not bring on his people the disaster he had threatened" (Exodus 32:11-14).

- "And Jesus said, 'Father, forgive them, for they know not what they do'" (Luke 23:34a).

*Dear God, you know I don't want to pray
for my offender.
I don't want you to bless him.
Help me to have a change of heart.*

Amen.

Chapter 9 Journal

Date: _____

_____

_____

_____

_____

_____

_____

_____

_____

_____

_____

_____

_____

_____

_____

_____

_____

_____

_____

_____

_____

_____

_____

_____

_____

_____

_____

_____

_____

_____

_____

_____

Part Five

Let the Journey Begin: The Steps of Forgiveness

Chapter 10
The Steps of Forgiveness: Part One

"The practice of forgiveness is our most important contribution to the healing of the world.[1]

Marianne Williamson

You may be ready to forgive and can hardly wait to take the first step. On the other hand, you may not want to forgive, but you choose to do so for your own physical, emotional, and spiritual wellbeing. Where do you begin? **The first step in *Moving from Broken to Beautiful® through Forgiveness* is to envision yourself breaking free from the bondage of unforgiveness.** The Israelites left the bondage of Egyptian slavery and embarked on a journey to the Promised Land. They complained and rebelled against the Lord. He punished them for their unbelief, and their journey dragged on in the desert for forty years. Like the Israelites, I complained and rebelled against the Lord. I didn't think I should have to forgive my ex-husband and recited all my reasons ad nauseam to God. It would be too hard. No one could expect me to forgive a jerk. Who could blame me for feeling the way I did after all he did to me?

How do you envision yourself breaking free from the bondage of unforgiveness?

I could have taken a first-class trip in breaking free from the bondage of unforgiveness. Instead I chose to drag on in the desert. Unlike the Israelites, I wore out my sandals as I kicked and stomped about the unfairness of it all. I coughed and sputtered as I breathed in the dry dusty air and moaned through parched lips.

How do you envision yourself breaking free from the bondage of unforgiveness? Will you wear your sandals and travel the dusty roads of a spiritual and emotional desert for forty years? Imagine if the ball and chain of unforgiveness could speak to you. They would say, "Life's such a drag. You've taken me on the dustiest roads, and you've stirred up my allergies."

Will you, as I did, drag on in the desert of unforgiveness or will you go first-class? The choice is yours.

The second step in *Moving from Broken to Beautiful® through Forgiveness* is to schedule time on your calendar to work on the steps of forgiveness. I have found that unless I schedule time for an activity or an event, I don't get to it. I may even forget it. My day fills with all kinds of things, good things but not necessarily the best.

The most effective method for me was to schedule time each day to work on the steps of forgiveness. Some women have told me they worked on forgiveness every day. Others have said they preferred every other day, a half-day twice a week, or a full day once a week. Choose what works best for you, but make a weekly plan to work on forgiveness and put it on your calendar. A friend may call you and say, "Let's go out for coffee or go to lunch on Wednesday."

Remember you are about to embark on a journey in moving from broken to beautiful through forgiveness. Schedule it on your calendar and protect it as best you can.

You look at your calendar first to make certain it's not during your scheduled forgiveness time. If it is, you can say, "I'm sorry, but I already have plans for that day."

And you do have plans, wonderful plans. You can always ask your friend to go a different day. Remember you are about to embark on a journey in moving from broken to beautiful through forgiveness. Schedule it on your calendar and protect it as best you can.

The third step in *Moving from Broken to Beautiful® through Forgiveness* is to read books on forgiveness. My counselor, my divorce recovery group, my Sunday school teacher, and my Bible study group recommended books on forgiveness. I didn't care if men or women wrote the books. It didn't matter if the books were long or short. The important thing was that reading felt safe. I would be by myself and didn't feel accountable to anyone. I didn't have to do anything except turn the pages, but God was at work. With every turn of the page, I sensed God urging me to let go of the bitterness, rage, anger, and unforgiveness.

How long do you want to be a prisoner of the person you refuse to forgive?

All the books basically said the same two things—I needed to let go of bitterness, rage, and anger and that forgiveness was for me. Without forgiveness, I would never be free from the person who hurt me. I wanted freedom and peace. The thought of being a prisoner of the person I refused to forgive was enough to make me work on forgiveness. No matter how hard forgiveness was, I would not be my ex-husband's prisoner.

Do you long for freedom and peace? How long do you want to be a prisoner of the person you refuse to forgive? How will you respond to God's prompting to let go of those negative emotions? Continue turning the pages of this book and then start turning the pages of other books about forgiveness.

Chapter 10 Activities

- Draw a picture of yourself breaking free from the bondage of unforgiveness. If you prefer, you can cut out pictures from a magazine.
- Schedule time on your calendar this week to work on forgiveness.
- Continue to read this book on forgiveness and do the activities.

Chapter 10 Affirmations

- Each day I am closer to freedom from the bondage of unforgiveness.
- I consider my work on forgiveness a sacred appointment on my calendar.
- I can check out books on forgiveness from a church library or borrow them from a friend.

Chapter 10 Reading and Prayer

- "Do not be afraid. Stand firm and you will see the deliverance the Lord will bring you today. The Egyptians [bondage] you see today you will never see again" (Exodus 14:13).
- "In the same way, faith by itself, if it is not accompanied by action, is dead" (James 2:17).
- "Plans fail for lack of counsel, but with many advisers they succeed" (Proverbs 15:22).

God, I admit I've struggled to forgive.
I don't think I'm in bondage.
But if I am, please help me
take that first step to forgive.

Amen.

Chapter 10 Journal   Date: _____

Yvonne Ortega

_____

_____

_____

_____

_____

_____

_____

_____

_____

_____

_____

_____

_____

_____

_____

Chapter 11
The Steps of Forgiveness: Part Two

"Forgiveness has nothing to do with absolving a criminal of his crime. It has everything to do with relieving oneself of the burden of being a victim--letting go of the pain and transforming oneself from victim to survivor."[1]

C.R. Strahan

The fourth step in *Moving from Broken to Beautiful® through Forgiveness* is to mourn offenses against you or your losses. I remember mourning the fact that I had given my ex-husband the best years of my life. I lost my youth, which should have been years of love, joy, and adventure. Instead I had lived in chaos, fear, and depression. I cried, journaled, talked about it in my divorce recovery group, and cried and journaled some more. Until I could express what I was specifically angry about, I couldn't release the pain and forgive my ex-husband.

According to a syndicated news column in 1934, Marshall Reid is credited with saying, "Time wounds all heels."[2] For a long time, I hoped he was right.

I wrote a letter to my ex-husband to tell him exactly how he hurt me and our child. I named specific dates and events. I spent a lot of time on that letter, but I didn't mail it to him. I read it to my counselor and parts of it to a trusted mentor. I'll explain later in this chapter why I didn't send it to my ex-husband.

If you are a widow, you may need to write a letter to your late husband about times he offended you that you resented. One widow said, "Yvonne, after he passed away, I realized he had been verbally abusive to me day after day. He belittled me and called me names."

> **You need to acknowledge the pain the offenses or losses caused you and the depth of that pain.**

You may be angry because your husband died and left you alone. A year after her husband died, one widow cried as she told me, "I'm angry he died. Why didn't he stick around and keep me company?"

Schedule that letter-writing time on your calendar and allow double the amount of time you expect it will take to write it. It usually takes longer than you think.

If your husband is dead, you can't read the letter to him. However, you can sit at his gravesite and read it aloud. Another option would be to read that letter to a trusted friend, a mentor, or a counselor.

If you are a survivor of childhood physical, emotional, or sexual abuse, you may have one or more abusers in your life. You can write a letter to each one to tell the person how he hurt you and wreaked havoc in your life. Then read that letter to a trustworthy friend, a mentor, or a counselor.

So why do you mourn your offenses or losses? You need to know exactly what you plan to forgive. Don't bury the pain. You need to acknowledge the pain those offenses or losses caused you and the depth of that pain. Once you voice it, you can continue moving from broken to beautiful through forgiveness.

If the offender is alive, you may wonder why you don't mail the letter to that person and why I didn't. R. T. Kendall answers that question, "I must add one caution: never go to a person you have had to forgive and say, 'I forgive you' . . . It is my experience that nine out of ten people I have had to forgive sincerely do not feel they have done anything wrong."[3]

The fifth step in *Moving from Broken to Beautiful® through Forgiveness* is to pour out your heart to God. Psalm 62:8 says, "Trust in him at all times, you people; pour out your hearts to him, for God is our refuge." I journaled every day and still do. I would go to the beach and sit with my Bible and journal. Through sniffles and sobs I would pour out my prayers, thoughts, heartaches, and victories to God. I told God without his help I could never forgive my ex-husband. The more I poured out my heart to God, the more I believed he was my refuge. I sensed God's presence, power, and passion to help me in moving from broken to beautiful through forgiveness.

How soon will it be before you pour out your heart to him? God loves you and longs to be your refuge. He wants to help you. Instead of writing in a journal, you may want to pour out your heart to God through artwork. One woman I know did that through her paintings. Another used colored chalk. You are the one doing this step of forgiveness. Choose a method that works for you.

Besides pouring out your heart to God, **the sixth step in *Moving from Broken to Beautiful® through Forgiveness* is to study the Bible, especially the life of Joseph.** Out of jealousy his brothers sold him into slavery. Years later, Joseph was second in command to Pharaoh, the king of Egypt. Joseph's brothers went to Egypt during the famine to buy food but didn't recognize him. Joseph identified himself, forgave them and said, "You intended to harm me, but God intended it for good to accomplish what is now being done, the saving of many lives" (Genesis 50:20).

Initially, I thought Joseph missed a great chance to get even with his brothers. I thought he should have fed only the innocent: his father and younger brother Benjamin.

Joseph said, "God sent me ahead of you to preserve for you a remnant on earth and to save your lives by a great deliverance" (Genesis 45:7). Why did he say that? After all, God didn't tell Joseph's brothers to sell him into slavery. However, God allowed them to do so and used it for good. Joseph did save the lives of his father, his brothers, their families and a remnant when they moved to Egypt during the famine.

Forgiveness is difficult, but it's for your benefit. What will you do so that God can bless you and your family the way he blessed Joseph and his family?

God didn't tell my ex-husband to abuse our child and me, but God allowed it. I didn't want to be a prisoner of the past or a victim paralyzed with self-pity. I let God use that domestic violence marriage and the divorce for good in my life and the lives of others and for his honor and glory. I longed for God to bless me and my family the way he blessed Joseph and his family. My son was part of my family, but part of my son's family was his father. If I wanted God's blessings, I would have to forgive my son's father and ask God to bless him too.

Forgiveness is difficult, but it's for your benefit. If you don't forgive, you can block God's blessings to you and your family.

Chapter 11 Activities

- Sit alone or with a friend and have a good cry over the offenses or losses in your life.
- Write about, draw, or paint a picture of you pouring your heart out.
- If you had a chance to talk to Joseph, what would you tell him or ask him?

Chapter 11 Affirmations

- I mourn the losses and offenses in my life with a safe person.
- Each day I pour out my heart to God.
- I learn from Joseph to forgive those who hurt me.

Chapter 11 Reading and Prayer

- "Blessed are those who mourn, for they will be comforted" (Matthew 5:4).
- "Heal me, Lord, and I will be healed; save me and I will be saved, for you are the one I praise" (Jeremiah 17:14).
- "The Lord is a refuge for the oppressed, a stronghold in times of trouble. Those who know your name trust in you, for you, Lord, have never forsaken those who seek you" (Psalm 9:9-10).

Dear God, please comfort and heal me.
I've suffered many losses and offenses.
Help me forgive as Joseph did.

Amen.

Chapter 11 Journal   Date: _____

_____

_____

_____

_____

_____

_____

_____

_____

_____

_____

_____

_____

_____

_____

_____

_____

_____

_____

_____

_____

_____

_____

_____

_____

_____

_____

_____

_____

_____

_____

Chapter 12
The Steps of Forgiveness: Part Three

"Many times, the decisions we make affect and hurt your closest
friends and family the most. I have a lot of regrets in that regard.
But God has forgiven me, which I am very thankful for.
It has enabled me to forgive myself and move forward one day
at a time."[1]

Lex Luger

**The seventh step in *Moving from Broken to
Beautiful® through Forgiveness* is to forgive
yourself.** If you are a survivor of childhood physical
abuse, it is not your fault. Regardless of what you did
wrong as a child, that didn't give your mother, father,
or both parents a reason to beat you with a belt, kick
you, punch you, burn you with cigarettes, or put you
on restriction for months at a time. They took their
anger, bitterness, and resentment over their problems
out on you. Please don't blame yourself for their
problems. Children will spill milk. Little ones may wet

the bed, but those are not deliberate vicious acts of disobedience that merit severe physical punishment. Maybe you didn't get all As and Bs in school, but that was not a reason to harm you physically.

You were the child. Your parents were the adults. They failed you, but it was not your fault. Be gentle with yourself and let go of the shame and guilt they imposed on you. Forgive yourself.

Please let go of the guilt and shame they imposed on you and forgive yourself for carrying that burden unnecessarily.

Perhaps you grew up with verbal abuse or neglect day after day. Your mother, father, or both parents may have called you filthy names, cursed at you, belittled you, or mocked you. Perhaps they abandoned you and lived for their job, their alcohol, or other drugs. That was not your fault either. They were out of control and needed professional help. You did not cause your parents to live unbalanced lives, to drink or use other drugs, or to neglect you. They allowed themselves to be driven to those things, and they didn't seek help. Perhaps they didn't realize they needed help because that is how they were raised.

You were the child. Your parents were the adults. They failed you. It was not your fault. Be gentle with yourself and let go of the shame and guilt they imposed on you. Forgive yourself for blaming yourself for years and the pain that caused you.

Maybe you suffered sexual abuse as a child. Perhaps your own father, an uncle, or a family friend molested you. It was not your fault no matter what he says. The perpetrator took advantage of your innocence and helplessness. The perpetrator may also have threatened to harm your family if you told what happened.

The sexual abuse was not your fault. Don't take on the shame and guilt that belong to the abuser. The abuser is the one who committed a crime and should go to jail.

Perhaps in anger or retaliation of the physical or sexual abuse, you said unkind things or did something immoral or illegal, please ask God for forgiveness and forgive yourself.

If you were in a domestic violence relationship, it was not your fault that the abuser battered you physically, emotionally, or any other way. Perhaps he told you, "The house isn't clean enough." Maybe he complained and said, "Dinner isn't good enough or ready on time." Maybe he said, "The children don't go to bed early enough." Those were excuses for the abuser to harm you. He found it easier to blame you rather than to look at himself and seek help for his problems. He said those things to maintain power and control.

Perhaps like me, you stayed too long in a domestic violence relationship and didn't leave until you saw the damage done to your child. Perhaps, as the result of the abuse you suffered, you hurt your child or children by being physically or verbally abusive.

Go through the steps of forgiveness to forgive yourself. Be sure to ask that child for forgiveness without making excuses. Also make amends. Your child may or may not forgive you. However, if you tell God you're sorry for your offenses, he forgives you. Since God has forgiven you, you have no reason to withhold forgiveness from yourself. If you do withhold it, it's as if you're telling God that he made a mistake by forgiving you. See my second book, *Moving from Broken to Beautiful: 9 Life Lessons to Help You Move Forward.* In Chapter 4, "Admit Your Mistakes," I cover my admission of guilt to my son. I did what I could to make amends and then needed to move forward for my sake and my son's.

A young man and his wife argued day and night for months and chose to separate to calm down for the sake of the children. While separated, the young man went out with old friends, got drunk, and had sex with one of the women. When he sobered up, he regretted his actions, cried, and called me. We prayed. He asked God to forgive him and asked for grace to forgive himself. He trusted God to answer both prayers. Today, he is once again a happy husband, father, and employee.

If your spouse was unfaithful, that was his choice. Perhaps your spouse ran from the hardships or problems of marriage and committed adultery as an escape. That was his choice. Perhaps he said, "It's not my fault. That pretty young gal at work threw herself at me."

Please don't destroy the rest of your life blaming yourself. Sherry Boykin says it well in her book, *But-Kickers: Growing Your Faith Bigger Than Your "But!"* "Where are the blood-washed, sanctified warriors who will fight for fidelity and stop blaming women for exciting passions that could just as easily be channeled into God's glory as into the gutter?"[2]

The eighth step in *Moving from Broken to Beautiful® through Forgiveness* is to play soft music. In *USA Today* on December 17, 2013, an article entitled "20 surprising, science-backed health benefits of music" appeared. Among some of the benefits, the article said that research suggests that music can ease pain, improve sleep quality, enhance blood vessel function, reduce stress, induce a meditative state, relieve symptoms of depression, elevate mood, and reduce anxiety as much as a massage.[3]

In the Old Testament King Saul was jealous of David and wanted to kill him. First Samuel 16:23 says, "David would take up his lyre [harp] and play. Then relief would come to Saul; he would feel better, and the evil spirit would leave him."

When I went through the divorce and again after a diagnosis of breast cancer, I played easy listening music or praise and worship music day and night. I experienced the benefits of music first-hand. When I struggled to forgive my ex-husband, music soothed my spirit and helped me to focus on my goal of health, peace, and freedom. When I received a diagnosis of breast cancer, I was angry with myself, God, the Food and Drug Administration, and the Environmental Protection Agency. Once again I experienced the benefits of music as I forgave God, those agencies, and myself. To read more about my experience with breast cancer, you can read my first book, *Finding Hope for Your Journey through Breast Cancer.*

The ninth step in *Moving from Broken to Beautiful® through Forgiveness* is to plan a new and better life. After the divorce was final, I returned to college and earned a master's degree in education to become a counselor. During my first year back in college, my professor encouraged the students to make a bucket list of 100 dreams. I made that list and became a Licensed Professional Counselor, a Licensed Substance Abuse Treatment Practitioner, and a Clinically Certified Domestic Violence Counselor. I kept working on my bucket list to plan a new and better life for myself. A diagnosis of breast cancer interrupted my dreams but didn't destroy them. Four car accidents in seven years caused further delays. Seven years ago, the loss of two aunts, my mother, and my only child within weeks of one another left me doubled over in gut-wrenching pain. All of those events meant something or someone else to forgive, but they also drove me to work harder on my new and better life. That led me to publish my second book, to become a Certified World Class Speaking Coach, and to allow more time for fun and laughter.

Take charge of your life. If you don't plan it and improve it, who will?

The highlight of my life came when I completed all 100 items on my list and made a new bucket list. I chose to focus on the future and not dwell on the past. What about you?

If you haven't made a plan for a new and better life, I encourage you to do so. Don't let the years slip by and drift from one year to the next. Take charge of your life. If you don't plan it and improve it, who will?

Chapter 12 Activities

- Journal about how you will forgive yourself because God has already forgiven you.
- Search on YouTube or in your favorite music store for easy listening music or praise and worship music to soothe your heart and soul.
- Make a list of your goals and dreams.

Chapter 12 Affirmations

- I forgive myself.
- I play soft music each day.
- I delight in my plan for a new and better life.

Chapter 12 Reading and Prayer

- "Truly I tell you, unless you change and become like little children, you will never enter the kingdom of heaven. Therefore, whoever takes the lowly position of this child is greatest in the kingdom of heaven. And whoever welcomes one such child in my name welcomes me" (Matthew 18:3-5).

- "Praise the LORD. Praise the LORD, my soul. I will praise the LORD all my life; I will sing praise to my God as long as I live" (Psalm 146:1-2).

- "There is surely a future hope for you, and your hope will not be cut off" (Proverbs 23:18).

*Dear God, help me to see myself as you do
and to understand how much you love me.
If I do, I can forgive myself.
Give me wisdom and discernment
to plan a new and better life.*

Amen.

Chapter 12 Journal   Date: _____

_____

_____

_____

_____

_____

_____

_____

_____

_____

_____

_____

_____

_____

_____

_____

_____

Yvonne Ortega

Appendix A: Additional Affirmations

- I'm thankful revenge is not my responsibility.
- I can forgive without seeking revenge.
- I know God will repay the offender.
- I won't pretend my spouse/partner treats me well if he doesn't.
- I won't cover up abuse.
- I don't make excuses for an abusive person.
- I demonstrate grace when I remember an offense and still forgive.
- I stay away from danger.
- I am a realist.
- I can be angry but not sin.
- I overcome the obstacles to forgiveness.
- I discuss my setbacks with a trustworthy person.
- I trust only those who earn my trust.
- I am neither naïve nor gullible.
- I recognize real sorrow.
- I let go of grievances.
- I can forgive even when the offender doesn't deserve it.
- I get rid of all bitterness and rage.
- I forgive just as in Christ God forgave me.
- I get rid of all malice.
- I treat others the way I want to be treated.
- I forgive to take care of my physical health.
- I avoid anxiety, stress, and depression through forgiveness.

- I choose peace rather than the bondage of unforgiveness.
- I move toward a 10 on the forgiveness scale.
- I pray for God to bless my enemies.
- I ask God to forgive my enemies as he forgives me.
- I travel first-class on the journey of forgiveness.
- I stay away from the desert of unforgiveness.
- I cherish my time to work on the steps of forgiveness.
- I receive the comfort I need.
- I sense God's presence and power.
- I forgive and receive blessings for me and my family.
- My hope will not be cut off.
- I see myself as God sees me.
- I play music to soothe my heart and soul.

Appendix B: Additional Readings

Chapter 1: Forgiveness Doesn't Mean the Person Gets away with Wrongdoing

- "And you may be sure that your sin will find you out" (Numbers 32:23b).
- "You [God] have set our iniquities before you, our secret sins in the light of your presence" (Psalm 90:8).
- "Woe to the wicked! Disaster is upon them! They will be paid back for what their hands have done" (Isaiah 3:11).

Chapter 2: Forgiveness Doesn't Mean You Minimize, Deny, or Rationalize What Happened

- "No one who practices deceit will dwell in my house; no one who speaks falsely will stand in my presence" (Psalm 101:7).
- "Do not lie. Do not deceive one another" (Leviticus 19:11b-c).
- "These are the things you are to do: Speak the truth to each other, and render true and sound judgment in your courts" (Zechariah 8:16).

Chapter 3: Forgiveness Doesn't Mean You Forget What Happened

- "But solid food is for the mature, who by constant use have trained themselves to distinguish good from evil" (Hebrews 5:14).
- "After this, Jesus went around in Galilee. He did not want to go about in Judea because the Jewish leaders there were looking for a way to kill him" (John 7:1).

- "If your brother or sister sins, go and point out their fault, just between the two of you. If they listen to you, you have won them over. But if they will not listen, take one or two others along, so that every matter may be established by the testimony of two or three witnesses. If they still refuse to listen, tell it to the church, and if they refuse to listen even to the church, treat them as you would a pagan or a tax collector" (Matthew 18:15-17).

Chapter 4: Forgiveness Doesn't Mean You Forgive the Person Right away

- "So watch yourselves. If your brother or sister sins against you, rebuke them; and if they repent, forgive them" (Luke 17:3).
- "If anyone has caused grief, he has not so much grieved me [Paul] as he has grieved all of you to some extent—not to put it too severely. The punishment inflicted on him by the majority is sufficient" (2 Corinthians 2:5-6).
- "You do not delight in sacrifice, or I would bring it; you do not take pleasure in burnt offerings. My sacrifice, O God, is a broken spirit; a broken and contrite heart you, God, will not despise" (Psalm 51:16-17).

Chapter 5: Forgiveness Doesn't Mean You Immediately Trust the Offender

- "Like a maniac shooting flaming arrows of death is one who deceives their neighbor and says, 'I was only joking!'" (Proverbs 26:18-19).

- "If a ruler listens to lies, all his officials become wicked" (Proverbs 29:12).
- "Leave your simple ways and you will live; walk in the way of insight. Whoever corrects a mocker invites insults; whoever rebukes the wicked incurs abuse. Do not rebuke mockers or they will hate you; rebuke the wise and they will love you. Instruct the wise and they will be wiser still; teach the righteous and they will add to their learning" (Proverbs 9:6-9).

Chapter 6: God Talks about Grievances

- "As a prisoner for the Lord, then, I urge you to live a life worthy of the calling you have received. Be completely humble and gentle; be patient, bearing with one another in love. Make every effort to keep the unity of the Spirit through the bond of peace" (Ephesians 4:1-3).
- "My dear brothers and sisters, take note of this: Everyone should be quick to listen, slow to speak, and slow to become angry, because human anger does not produce the righteousness that God desires" (James 1:19-20).
- "Then the master called the servant in. 'You wicked servant,' he said, 'I canceled all that debt of yours because you begged me to. Shouldn't you have had mercy on your fellow servant just as I had on you?'" (Matthew 18:32-33).

Chapter 7: God Talks about Bitterness

- "See to it that no one falls short of the grace of God and that no bitter root grows up to cause trouble and defile many" (Hebrews 12:15-16).

- "What causes fights and quarrels among you? Don't they come from your desires that battle within you? You desire but do not have, so you kill. You covet but you cannot get what you want, so you quarrel and fight. You do not have because you do not ask God" (James 4:1-2).

- "But now you must also rid yourselves of all such things as these: anger, rage, malice, slander, and filthy language from your lips" (Colossians 3:8).

Chapter 8: The Self-defeating Sacrifice of Unforgiveness

- "May I wholeheartedly follow your decrees, that I may not be put to shame" (Psalm 119:80).

- "Refrain from anger and turn from wrath; do not fret—it leads only to evil. For those who are evil will be destroyed, but those who hope in the LORD will inherit the land" (Psalm 37:8-9).

- "Walk with the wise and become wise, for a companion of fools suffers harm" (Proverbs 13:20).

Chapter 9: Where Are You on the Forgiveness Scale?

- "Do not rejoice when your enemy falls, and let not your heart be glad when he stumbles" (Proverbs 24:17 ESV).
- "If you find your enemy's ox or donkey loose, take it back to him. If you see the donkey of someone who hates you lying helpless under its load, don't walk off and leave it. Help it up" (Exodus 23:5 Message).
- "When a man's ways please the LORD, he makes even his enemies to be at peace with him" (Proverbs 16:7).

Chapter 10: The Steps of Forgiveness: Part One

- "Let the morning bring me word of your unfailing love, for I have put my trust in you. Show me the way I should go, for to you I entrust my life" (Psalm 143:8).
- "There is a time for everything, and a season for every activity under the heavens" (Ecclesiastes 3:1).
- "Do not be deceived: God cannot be mocked. A man reaps what he sows. Whoever sows to please their flesh, from the flesh will reap destruction; whoever sows to please the Spirit, from the Spirit will reap eternal life" (Galatians 6:7-8).

Chapter 11: The Steps of Forgiveness: Part Two

- "Weeping may endure for a night, but joy comes in the morning" (Psalm 30:5, NKJV).
- "Praise be to the God and Father of our Lord Jesus Christ, the Father of Compassion

and the God of all comfort, who comforts us in all our troubles, so that we can comfort those in any trouble with the comfort we ourselves receive from God" (2 Corinthians 1:3-4).

- "But while Joseph was there in the prison, the LORD was with him; he showed him kindness and granted him favor in the eyes of the prison warden. So the warden put Joseph in charge of all those held in the prison, and he was made responsible for all that was done there. The warden paid no attention to anything under Joseph's care, because the LORD was with Joseph and gave him success in whatever he did" (Genesis 39:20c-23).

Chapter 12: The Steps of Forgiveness: Part Three

- "If anyone causes one of these little ones—those who believe in me—to stumble, it would be better for them to have a large millstone hung around their neck and to be drowned in the depths of the sea. Woe to the world because of the things that cause people to stumble! Such things must come, but woe to the person through whom they come" (Matthew 18:6-7)!

- "Praise the LORD . . . Praise him with the sounding of the trumpet, praise him with the harp and lyre, praise him with timbrel and dancing, praise him with the strings and pipe, . . . Let everything that has breath praise the LORD. Praise the LORD" (Psalm 150:1a, 3-4, 6).

- "The Lord will guide you always; he will satisfy your needs in a sun-scorched land and will strengthen your frame. You will be like a well-watered garden, like a spring whose waters never fail" (Isaiah 58:11).

Conclusion

I still don't have forgiveness totally conquered. Every now and then I think an eye for an eye and a tooth for a tooth might not be a bad idea. I'm glad everyone else doesn't feel that way, or this world would be full of blind, toothless people.

I'll never forget what happened in my marriage. So I'll work on forgiveness until I die, but thank God I'm not where I used to be. I'm no longer the queen of anger. I gave up that position and recommend that you not take it on. I no longer blame all men for what one man did. That would be as foolish as a man blaming all women for what one woman did to him.

What God taught me is that forgiveness is a process, and that's OK. It's what keeps me going back to him. Almost every time a memory surfaces, my hurt rises again and I feel like I'm starting over. Like the geraniums on my patio, when the leaves dry out and the blooms shrivel, I have to pull them out so that new blooms can come.

It's the same with me. I have to let God remove toxic feelings of bitterness, rage, and anger if I want to experience his renewal and peace and live free. One thing I know for sure is that I worked hard to forgive my ex-husband, and I have forgiven him. I pray for him on my own without God telling me to do so. I wish him, his second wife, and their child God's best.

I knew I had moved forward in forgiveness when my son called me to pray for his dad. He said, "Dad has cancer, Mom. Please pray for him."

"I pray for him every day, honey."

"I know you do, Mom. That's why I called you."

My son called me when his stepmother got cancer and asked me to pray for her, and I did.

I have moved from broken to beautiful through forgiveness. It wasn't easy, but I cherish God's renewal and peace and live free at last.

How eager are you to experience God's renewal and peace and live a life of freedom? If you have not yet surrendered to the process of forgiveness to make that life possible, when will you do it?

I pray that God blesses you richly in moving from broken to beautiful through forgiveness. I look forward to hearing from you and how your life has changed for the better. You can contact me through my website at www.yvonneortega.com or through my email at yvonne@yvonneortega.com

Notes

Chapter 1

[1]www.quotationspage.com/quote/38001.html.
[2]*Psychology Today,* September 15, 2013.
https://www.psychologytoday.com/blog/pieces-mind/201309/revenge-will-you-feel-better

Chapter 2

[1]www.brainyquote.com/quotes/quotes/b/bernard
mel132866.html.
[2]R.T. Kendall, *Total Forgiveness Revised and Updated* (Lake Mary, FL: Charisma House, 2002, 2007), Used by permission, 23.
[3]Beth Moore, *Children of the Day* (Nashville, TN: LifeWay, 2014 Reprinted and used by permission), 42.

Chapter 3

[1]www.brainyquote.com/quotes/quotes/l/lewisbsm
e132879.html.
[2]Beth Moore, *Breaking Free: Making Liberty in Christ a Reality in Life* (Nashville, TN: LifeWay, 1999 Reprinted and used by permission), 104.
[3]R.T. Kendall, *Total Forgiveness Revised and Updated* (Lake Mary, FL: Charisma House, 2002, 2007), Used by permission, 29.

Chapter 4

[1]http://www.huffingtonpost.com/dr-tian-dayton/forgiveness-is-a-verb_b_2940722.html.

[2]174.136.95.244/you/sermon-
outlines/content/?topic=anger_and_forgiveness
[3]http://www.huffingtonpost.com/dr-tian-
dayton/forgiveness-is-a-verb_b_2940722.html.
[4]http://www.whatchristianswanttoknow.com/bible
-verses-about-patience-20-scripture-
quotes/#ixzz3bewScnvV

Chapter 5

[1]www.goodreads.com/quotes/tag/forgiveness

Chapter 6

[1]www.inspirationalstories.com

Chapter 7

[1]www.brainyquote.com/quotes/keywords/bitterne
ss.html.

Chapter 8

[1] www.goodreads.com/quotes/tag/forgive

Chapter 9

[1]http://www.goodreads.com/authorshow/3565.os
car_wilde

Chapter 10

[1]www.goodreads.com/**quotes**/tag/**forgiveness**

Chapter 11

[1]www.goodreads.com/**quotes**/tag/**forgiveness**
[2]www.quoteinvestigator.com/2014/09/23/heels/
[3]R.T. Kendall, *Total Forgiveness Revised and Updated* (Lake Mary, FL: Charisma House, 2002, 2007), Used by permission, 76.

Chapter 12

[1]www.brainyquote.com/quotes/topics/topic_forgiveness.html#rEDAHCXj0XiLs1HJ.99
[2]Sherry Boykin, *But-Kickers: Growing Your Faith Bigger Than Your "But!"* (Clarks Summit, PA: But-Kickers Books, 2015 Reprinted and used by permission), 39.
[3]*USA Today*, December 17, 2013.
http://www.usatoday.com/story/news/health/2013/12/17/health-benefits-music/4053401/

About The Author

Yvonne Ortega is a Licensed Professional Counselor, a Licensed Substance Abuse Treatment Practitioner, and a Clinically Certified Domestic Violence Counselor. She is the author of *Moving from Broken to Beautiful: 9 Life Lessons to Help You Move Forward* (Crystal Pointe Media, Inc.), *Finding Hope for Your Journey through Breast Cancer* (Revell) and a contributing author to *The Embrace of a Father* (Bethany House) and *Transformed* (Wine Press). She has presented writers' workshops from coast to coast in the USA and received a literary award at the Maine Fellowship of Christian Writers in 2002. She also received the Persistence Award at the American Christian Writers Conference in Virginia in 2002 for continuing to write during the time of aggressive treatment for cancer. As a survivor of domestic violence, breast cancer, and the loss of her only child, she loves to speak to audiences about her journey in Moving from Broken to Beautiful® through Forgiveness. Yvonne is also a Certified World Class Speaking Coach. She regularly conducts compelling, uplifting, interactive keynotes, workshops, seminars, and retreats for women who wear anything from designer suits to jumpsuits. You can reach Yvonne at www.yvonneortega.com She enjoys connecting with her readers through her website blog and through email at yvonne@yvonneortega.com.

She has spoken in English for such organizations as cancer support groups, churches, Kairos Prison

Ministry, the Peninsula Women's Network, NSA (National Speakers Association) Virginia Chapter Pro Track Speakers Academy, Stonecroft Ministries, the Virginia Breast Cancer Foundation Peninsula Chapter, Hope for the Journey, and Women of Value in Every Nation in Richmond, Virginia. She has spoken in Spanish in New Jersey for Stonecroft Ministries and at a Spanish retreat for Olive Grove Church in Nuevo, CA.

Her hobbies are walking at the beach, collecting shells, listening to the waves, reading and traveling. Exercise and proper nutrition also play a part in her life.

Connect with
Yvonne Ortega

Yvonne's website:
www.yvonneortega.com

Blog: home page of website

Facebook: Yvonne Ortega

Twitter: @yvonneortega1

Linkedin: Yvonne Ortega

YouTube Channel: yvonneortega01

Cancer isn't the last word. Hope is.

80 Inspirational Readings

Finding Hope
for
Your Journey
through
Breast Cancer

Yvonne Ortega

"A wonderfully honest and uplifting book. Those who walk through the valley of the shadow of cancer no longer have to travel alone."

Donna Partow, Author, *Becoming the Woman I Want to Be*

Revell
a division of Baker
Publishing Group
www.RevellBooks.com

Available on Kindle
Signed paperback
available from
the author

Turn your trial into triumph.
You too can move forward.

"Being true to ourselves is sometimes one of the more difficult challenges in life. This easy to read, interactive book helps open our hearts and minds to truths we may have overlooked and helps propel us to a place of wholeness."

Dr. Thelma Wells (Mama T), CEO, That A Girl and Friends Speakers Agency and That A Girl Enrichment Tours, Author and Speaker

| Crystal Pointe Media, Inc. | Available on Kindle |
| www.crystalpointemedia.com | Signed paperback available from the author |

Made in the USA
Charleston, SC
22 May 2016